Yellowstone National Park Adult Coloring Book

Preston Guymon

ISBN-10: 1517744377
ISBN-13: 978-1517744373

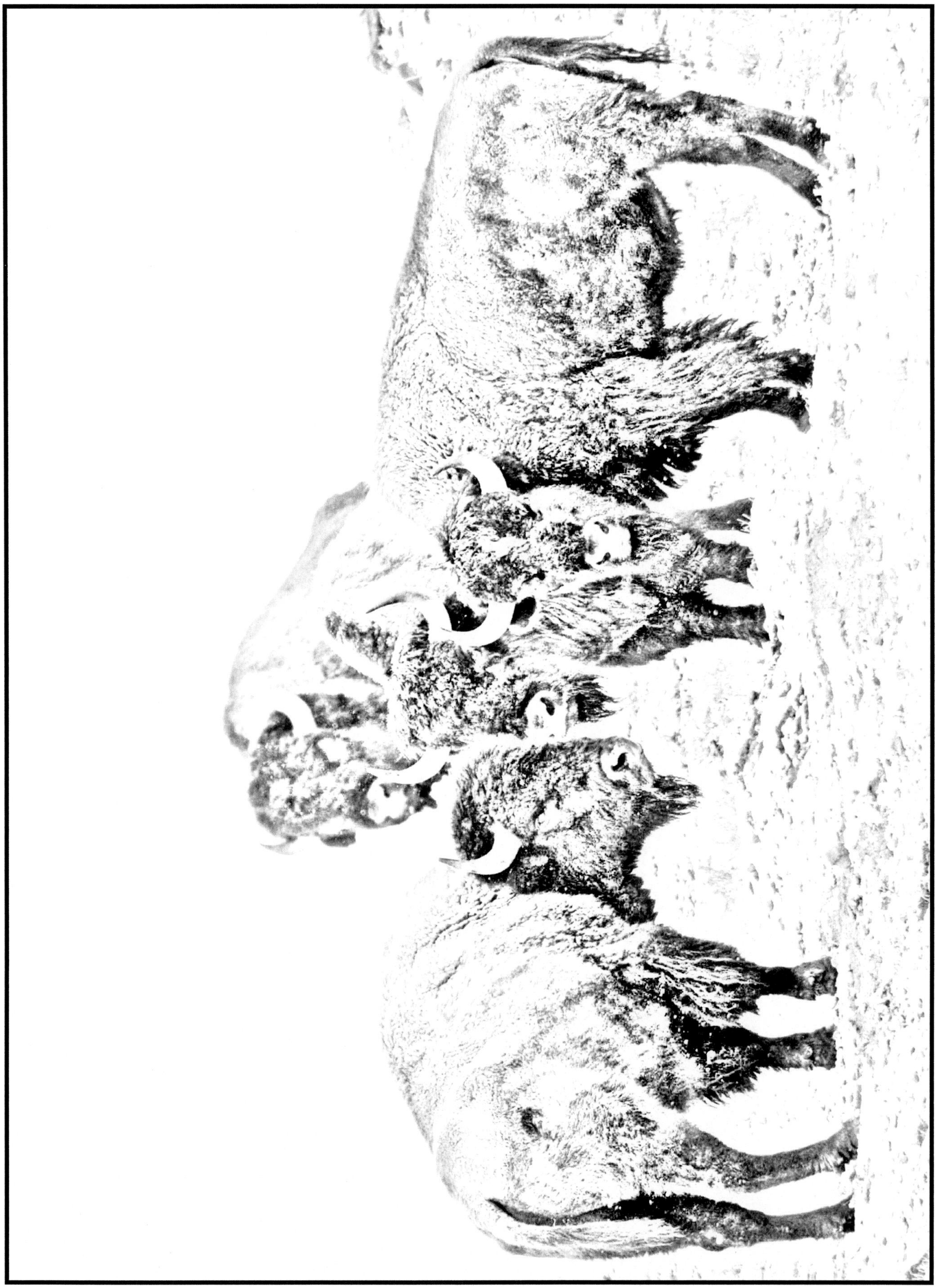

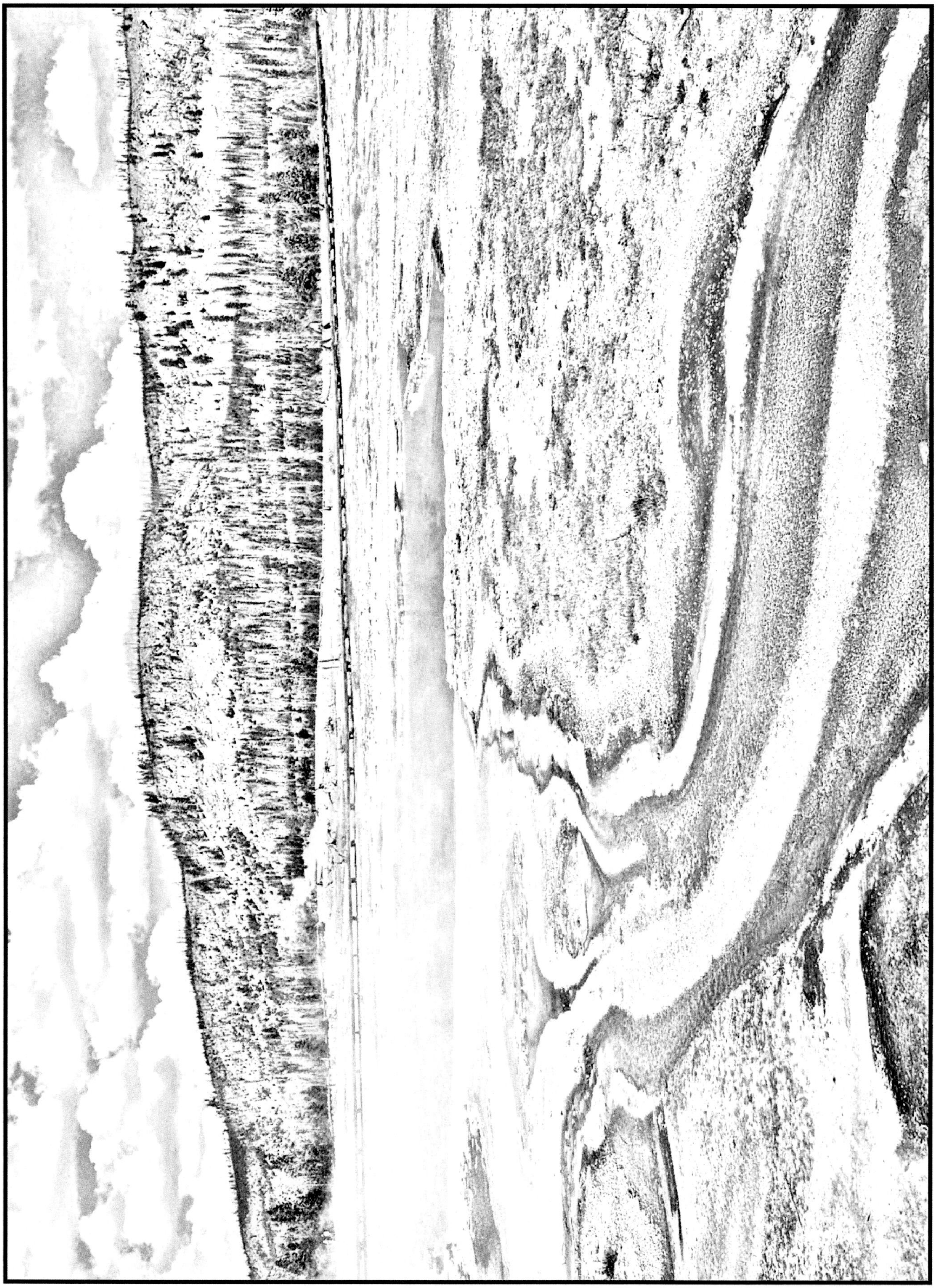

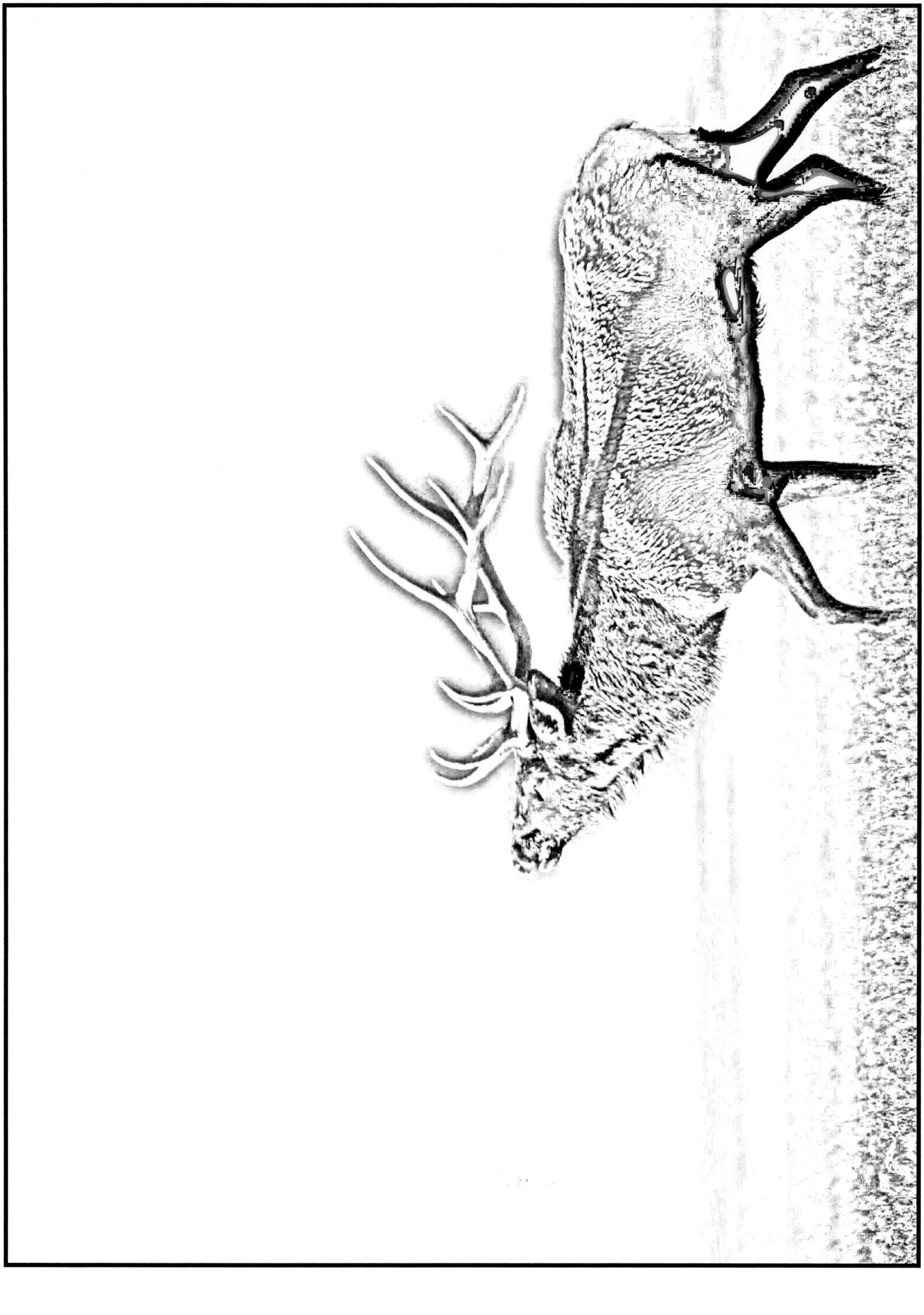

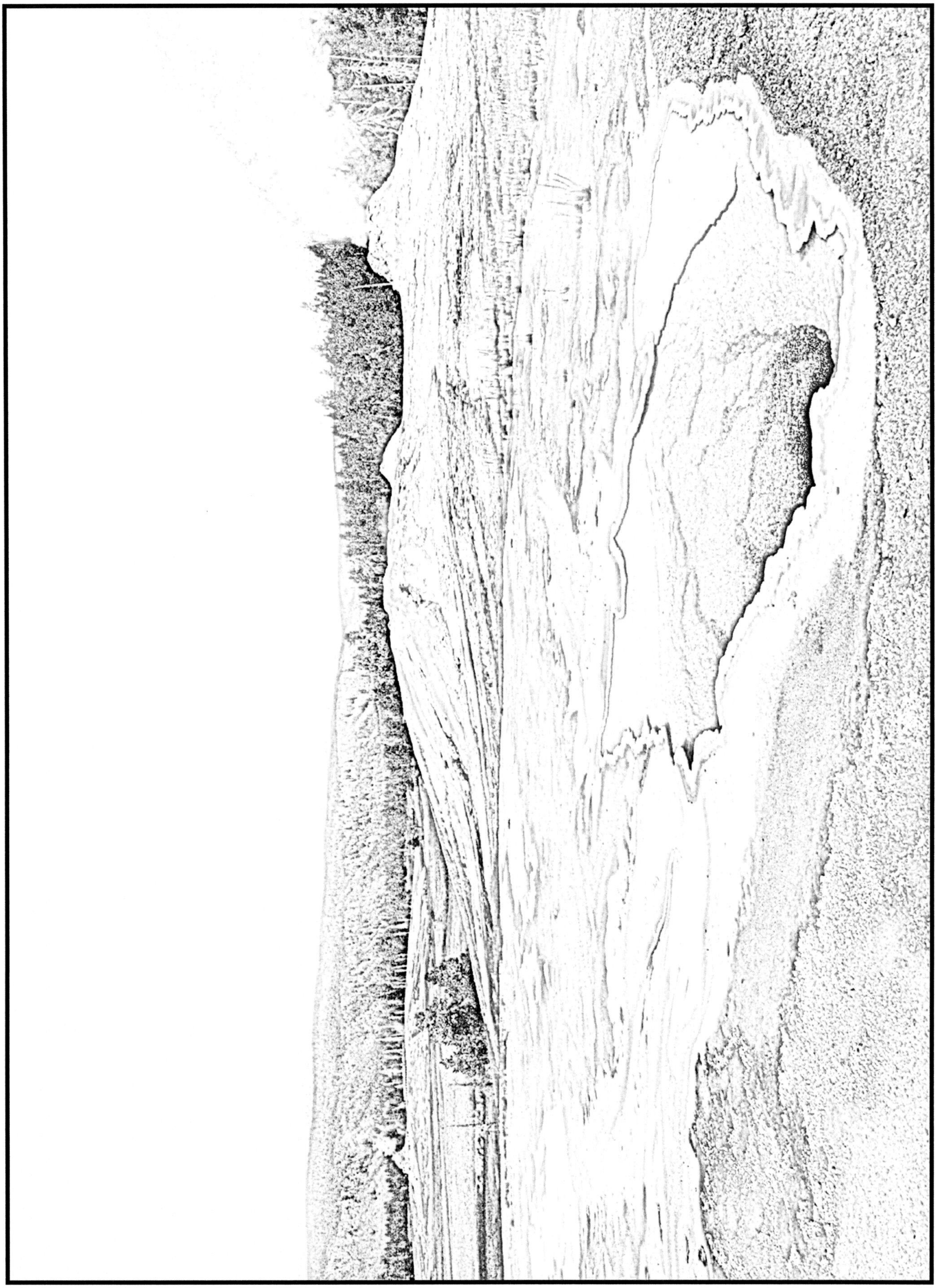

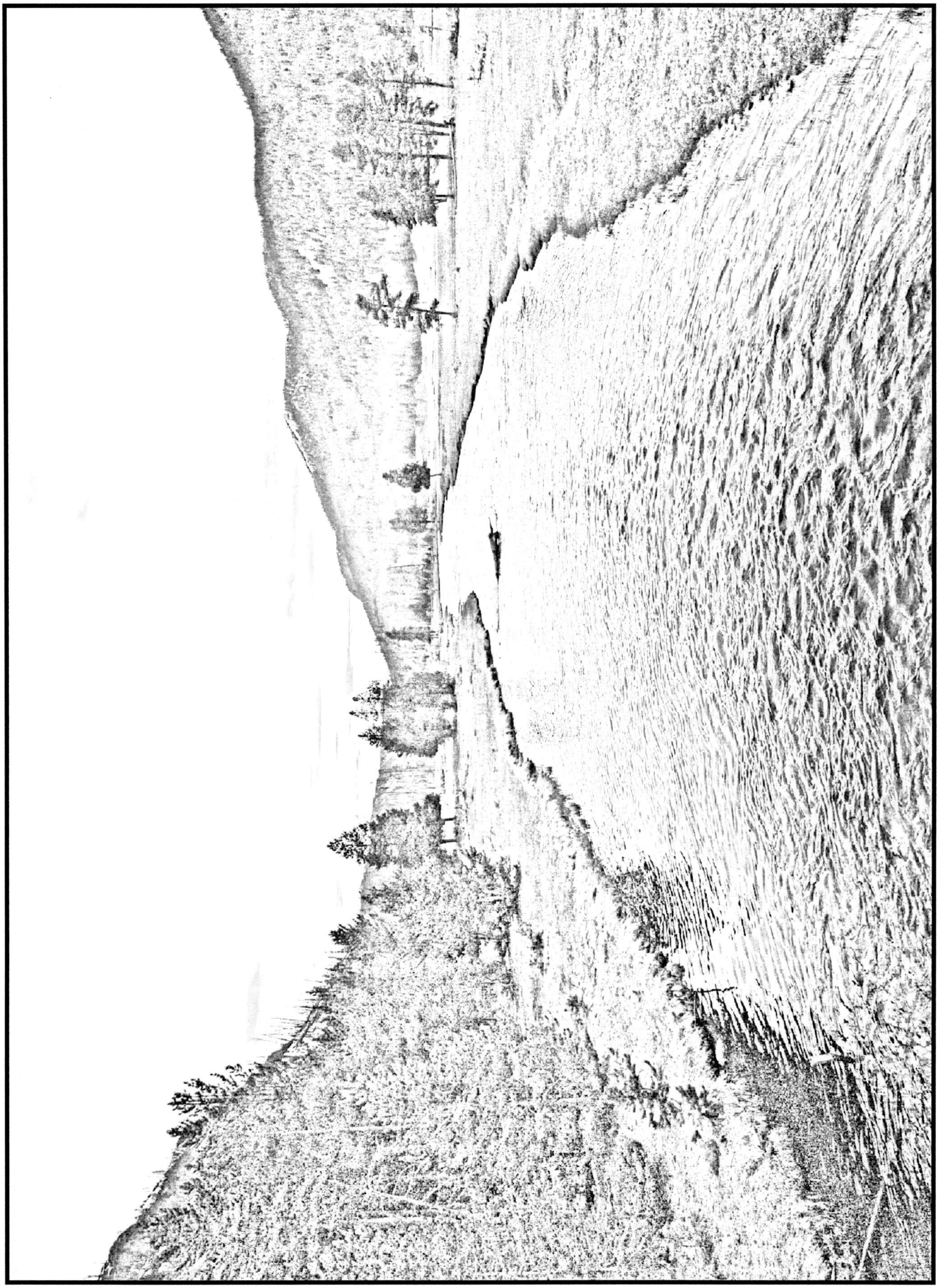

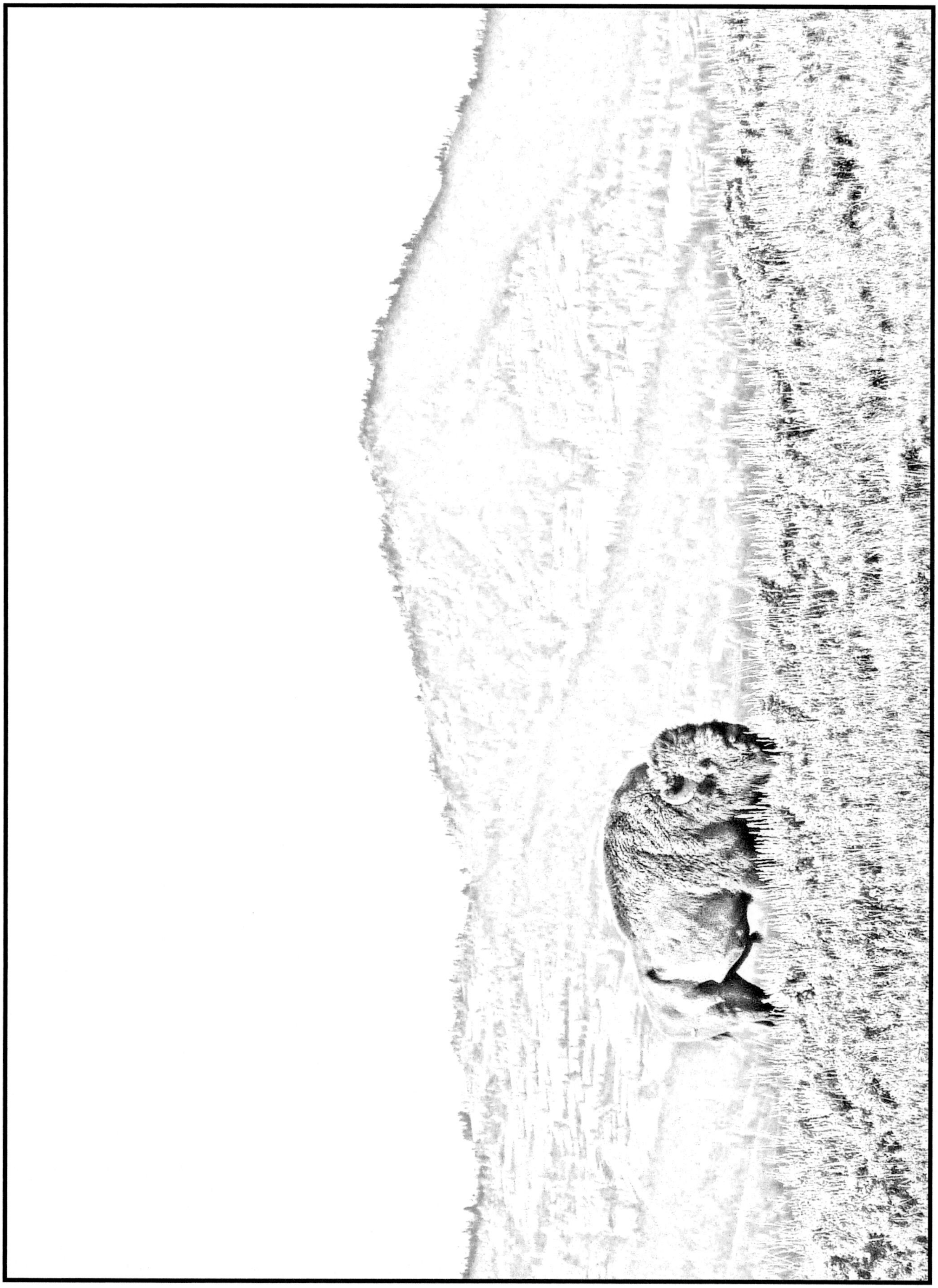

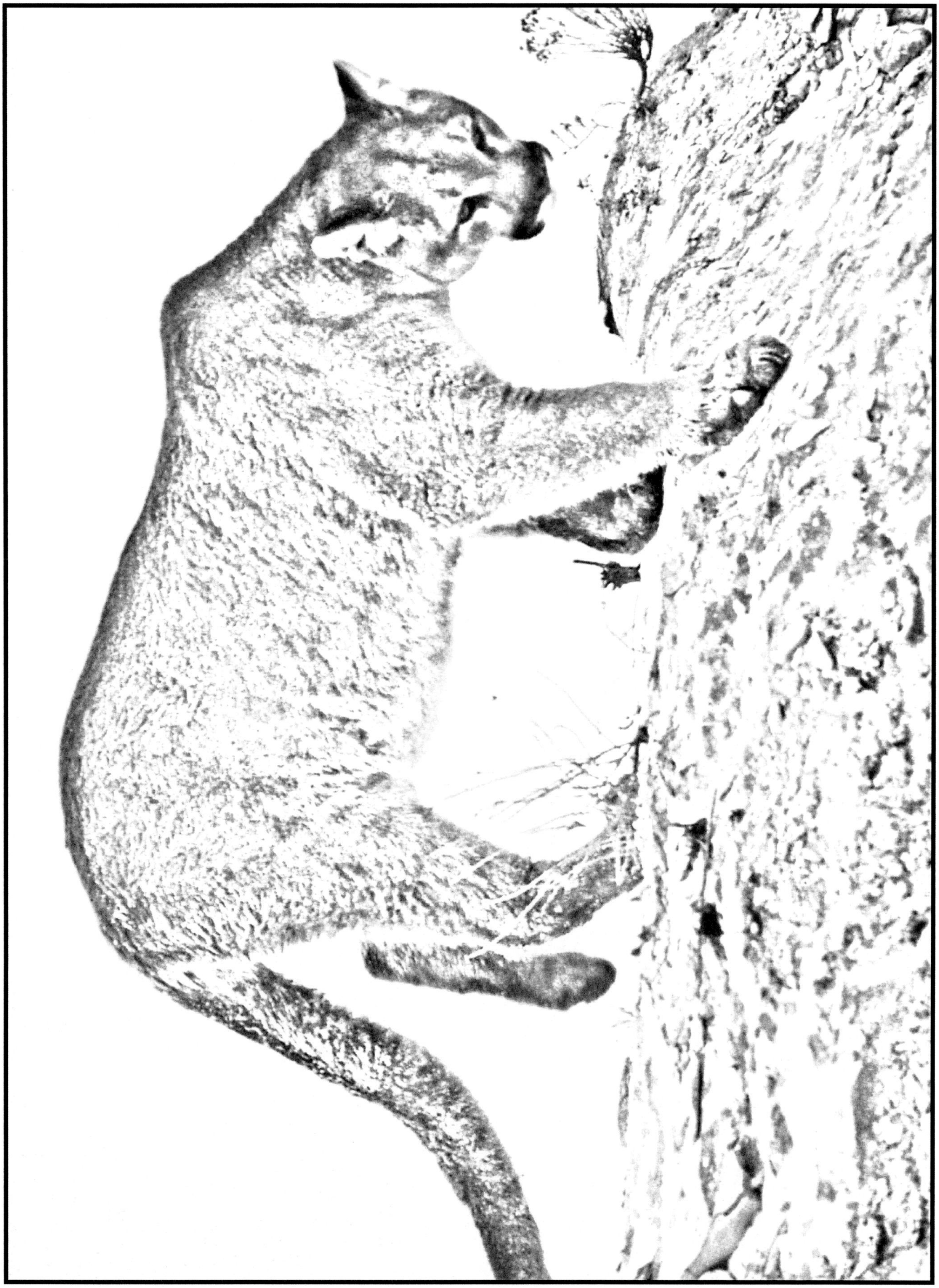

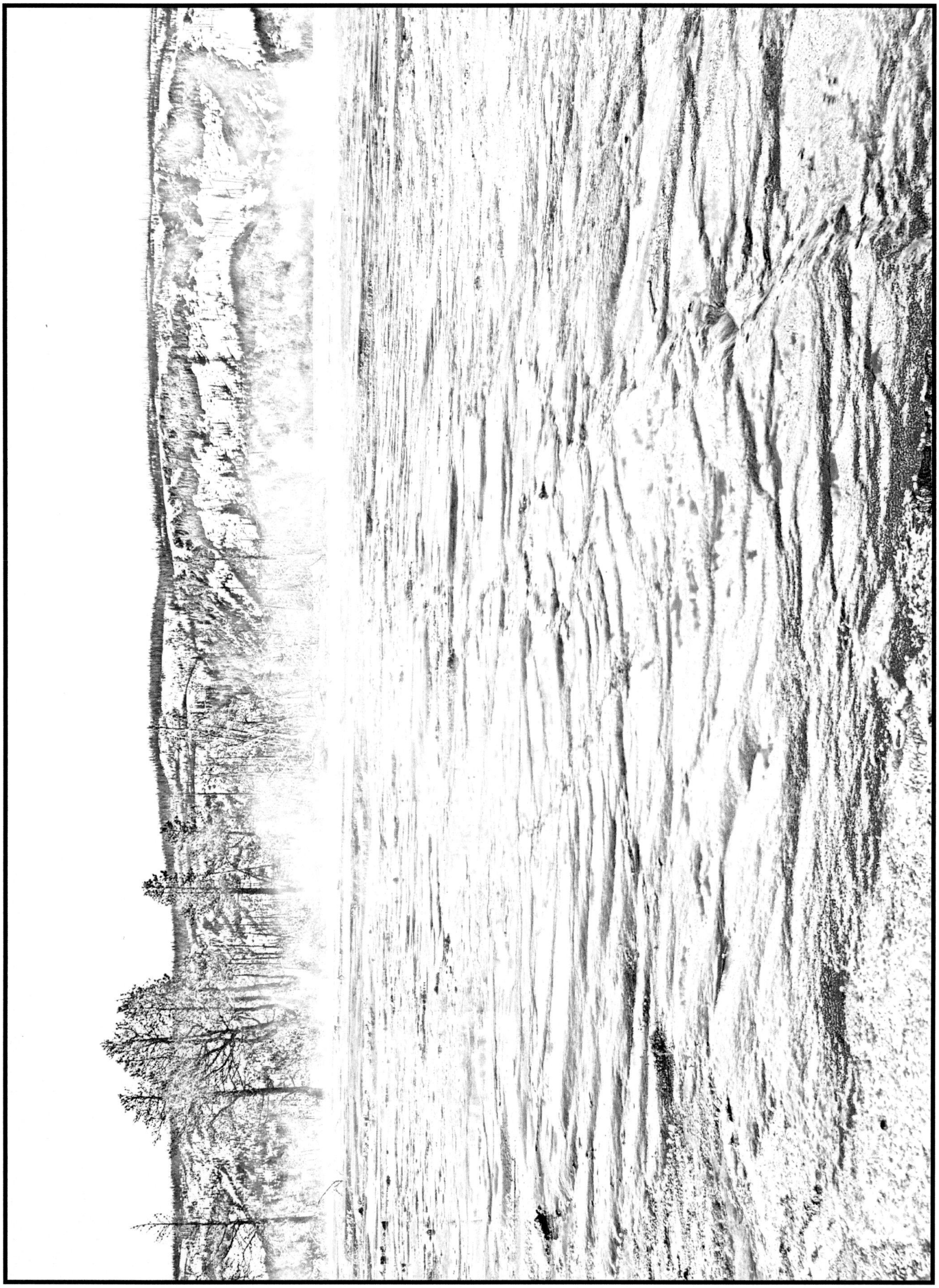

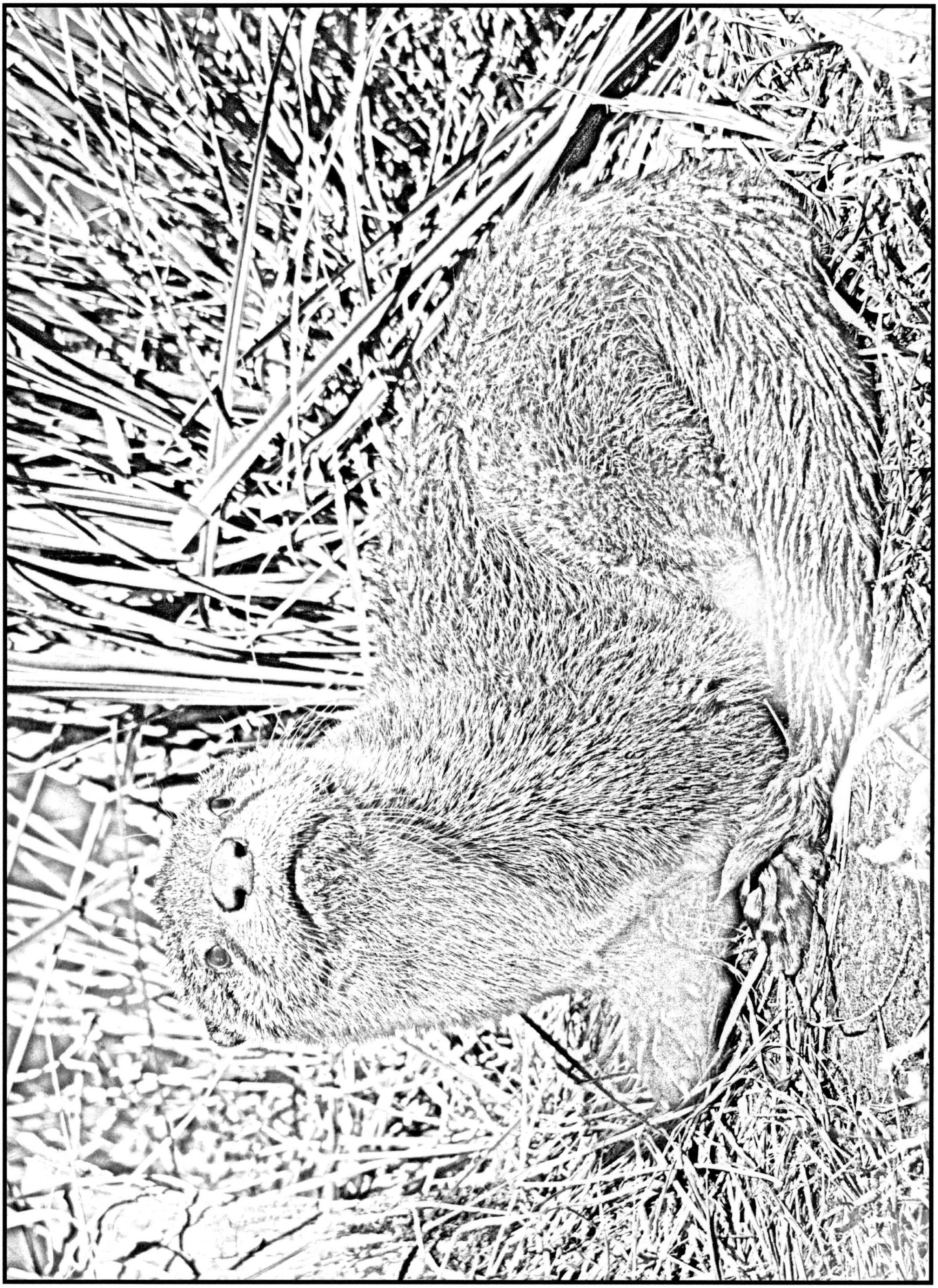

36000244R00030

Made in the USA
San Bernardino, CA
10 July 2016